to

_____

from

_____

FAMILY
CHRISTIAN
PRESS

teens

RADICAL
DEVOTIONS
FOR
Girlfriends

teens

RADICAL
DEVOTIONS
FOR
Girlfriends

Table of Contents

Introduction

Okay, girlfriend, it's time to face facts: Jesus was radical . . . *extremely* radical. He came to earth in a radical way. He did radical things; He made radical claims; and He asked His followers to make radical changes in their lives. And that's either good news or bad news, depending on how you look at it.

If you'd prefer to be a "Sunday-only" Christian who keeps Christ at a "safe" distance, then the idea of a radical Jesus isn't too pleasant to think about. But, if you're looking for something more than one-day-a-week Christianity, if you're searching for a faith that's 24-7, then the idea of following a radical Jesus isn't really a sacrifice at all—it's a blessing.

This book of devotionals can help you think about the radical changes that your relationship with Christ can—and should— make in your life. This text contains 31 devotional readings of particular interest to young women like you, women who have a sincere desire to grow in their faith. Each chapter contains Bible verses, a brief devotional reading, quotations from noted Christian women, and a prayer.

Are you willing to form a radical relationship with Jesus? And do you desire the eternal abundance and peace that can be yours through Him? If so, ask for God's help and ask for it many times each day . . . starting with a regular, heartfelt devotional—a regular, *radical* devotional.

Chapter 1

Are You Radical?

You were taught to leave your old self—to stop living the evil way you lived before. That old self becomes worse, because people are fooled by the evil things they want to do. But you were taught to be made new in your hearts, to become a new person. That new person is made to be like God—made to be truly good and holy.

Ephesians 4:22-24 NCV

When it comes to your faith, are you "radical" or "run-of-the-mill"? Is your life radically different because of your relationship with Jesus, or are you the same person you were *before* you invited Him into your life?

Jesus wants to have a radical, life-altering relationship with you. Are you willing to have a radical relationship with Him? Unless you can answer this question with a resounding "Yes," you will rob yourself of the abundance that can and should be yours through Christ.

Ruth Bell Graham observed, "God's work is not in buildings, but in transformed lives." Are you a transformed person because of your relationship with the One from Galilee? Hopefully so. When you invited Christ to reign over your heart, you became a radically new creation. This day offers yet another opportunity to behave yourself like that new person. When you do, God will guide your steps and bless your endeavors . . . forever.

God gives to us a heavenly gift called joy,
radically different in quality from any natural joy.

Elisabeth Elliot

When we give ourselves wholly to God,
He takes from our meager reserves and
gives back from infinity.
What a marvelous exchange!

Shirley Dobson

God wants to teach us that when we commit
our lives to Him, He gives us
that wonderful teacher, the Holy Spirit.

Gloria Gaither

Thought for the Day

Jesus Made a Radical Sacrifice for You . . .

What kind of sacrifice
are you willing to make for Him?

More Words from God's Word

So let's keep focused on that goal [reaching out to Christ], those of us who want everything God has for us. If any of you have something else in mind, something less than total commitment, God will clear your blurred vision, you'll see it yet!

Philippians 3:15-16 MSG

Don't look for shortcuts to God. The market is flooded with surefire, easygoing formulas for a successful life that can be practiced in your spare time. Don't fall for that stuff, even though crowds of people do. The way to life—to God!—is vigorous and requires total attention.

Matthew 7:13-14 MSG

Now I Pray

Lord, You have created a glorious universe, and You have created me. Let me become radically committed to You and to Your son.

Amen

Chapter 2

Are You Different?

If anyone belongs to Christ,
there is a new creation.
The old things have gone;
everything is made new!

2 Corinthians 5:17 NCV

Okay, girlfriend, answer this question *honestly*: Do you behave differently because of your relationship with Jesus? Or do you behave in pretty much the same way that you would if you *weren't* a believer? Hopefully, the fact that you've invited Christ to reign over your heart means that you've made BIG changes in your thoughts *and* your actions.

Doing the right thing is not always easy, especially when you're tired or frustrated. But, doing the *wrong* thing almost always leads to trouble. And sometimes, it leads to *big* trouble.

If you're determined to follow "the crowd," you may soon find yourself headed in the wrong direction. So here's some advice: Don't follow the crowd—follow Jesus. And keep following Him every day of your life.

It is tempting to imagine that,
given a different lot in life, circumstances
other than those in which we find ourselves,
we would make much greater strides in holiness.
The truth is that the place where we are is
God's schoolroom, not somewhere else.
Here we may be conformed
to the likeness of Christ.

Elisabeth Elliot

Do nothing that you would not like to be doing
when Jesus comes. Go no place where you
would not like to be found when He returns.

Corrie ten Boom

Thought for the Day

Trust Your Conscience:
That little voice inside your head will guide
you down the right path if you listen carefully.
Very often, your conscience will actually tell you
what God wants you to do. So listen, learn,
and behave accordingly.

More Words from God's Word

Do what God's teaching says;
when you only listen and do nothing,
you are fooling yourselves.

James 1:22 NCV

And we pray this in order that you may live
a life worthy of the Lord and may please him
in every way: bearing fruit in every good work,
growing in the knowledge of God.

Colossians 1:10 NIV

Now I Pray

Lord, the life that I live and the words
that I speak will tell the world how
I feel about You. Today and every day,
let my testimony be worthy of You.
Let my words be sure and true,
and let my actions point others to You.
Amen

Chapter 3

God's Love Is Perfect

(So You Don't Have to Be)

Whoever is wise will observe these things,
and they will understand
the lovingkindness of the LORD.

Psalm 107:43 NKJV

You live in a world where expectations are high, incredibly high, or unreachable. The media delivers an endless stream of messages that tell you how to look, how to behave, how to eat, and how to dress. The media's expectations are impossible to meet—God's are not. God doesn't expect you to be perfect . . . and neither should you.

If you find yourself bound up by the chains of perfectionism, it's time to ask yourself who you're trying to impress, and why. If you're trying to impress other people, it's time to reconsider your priorities.

Remember this: the expectations that *really* matter are not society's expectations or your friends' expectations. The expectations that matter are God's expectations, pure and simple. And everything else should take a back seat.

So do your best to please God, and don't worry too much about what other people think. And, when it comes to meeting the unrealistic expectations of our crazy world, forget about trying to meet those unrealistic expectations and concentrate, instead, on living a life that's pleasing to God.

God is so inconceivably good.
He's not looking for perfection.
He already saw it in Christ.
He's looking for affection.

Beth Moore

Excellence is not perfection,
but essentially a desire to be strong in the Lord
and for the Lord.

Cynthia Heald

Face your deficiencies and acknowledge them;
but do not let them master you. Let them teach
you patience, sweetness, insight.
When we do the best we can,
we never know what miracle is wrought
in our life, or in the life of another.

Helen Keller

Thought for the Day

Don't Be Too Hard on Yourself:
You don't have to be perfect
to be wonderful.

More Words from God's Word

Those who wait for perfect weather will never plant seeds; those who look at every cloud will never harvest crops. Plant early in the morning, and work until evening, because you don't know if this or that will succeed. They might both do well.

Ecclesiastes 11:4,6 NCV

Your beliefs about these things should be kept secret between you and God. People are happy if they can do what they think is right without feeling guilty.

Romans 14:22 NCV

Now I Pray

Lord, this world has so many expectations of me, but today I will not seek to meet the world's expectations; I will do my best to meet Your expectations. I will make You my ultimate priority, Lord, by serving You, by praising You, by loving You, and by obeying You.

Amen

Chapter 4

Whose Footsteps Are You Following?

Whoever serves me must follow me.
Then my servant will be with me everywhere I am.
My Father will honor anyone
who serves me.

John 12:26 NCV

everybody on planet Earth serves somebody or something—and you're no exception. Either you will serve God (by following His Son) or not. And in the final analysis, whom you serve determines whom you become.

Who are you going to walk with today? Are you going to walk with people who worship the ways of the world? Or are you going to walk with the Son of God? Jesus walks with you. Are you walking with Him? Hopefully, you will choose to walk with Him today and every day of your life.

Today provides another glorious opportunity to place yourself in the service of the One from Galilee. May you seek His will, may you trust His Word, and may you walk in His footsteps—now and forever—amen.

The Christian faith is meant to be lived
moment by moment. It isn't some broad,
general outline—it's a long walk with
a real Person. Details count: passing thoughts,
small sacrifices, a few encouraging words,
little acts of kindness,
brief victories over nagging sins.

Joni Eareckson Tada

You cannot cooperate with Jesus in
becoming what He wants you to become and
simultaneously be what the world desires
to make you. What will it be?
The world and you, or Jesus and you?
You do have a choice to make.

Kay Arthur

Thought for the Day

If You Want to Be a Disciple of Christ . . .
follow in His footsteps,
obey His commandments,
and share His never-ending love.

More Words from God's Word

"Follow Me," He told them,
"and I will make you fishers of men!"
Immediately they left their nets
and followed Him.

Matthew 4:19-20 HCSB

The LORD has already told you what is good,
and this is what he requires: to do what is right,
to love mercy, and to walk humbly
with your God.

Micah 6:8 NLT

Now I Pray

Dear Jesus, because I am Your disciple,
I will trust You, I will obey Your teachings,
and I will share Your Good News. You have
given me life abundant and life eternal,
and I will follow You today and forever.
Amen

Chapter 5

Is the Golden Rule Your Rule, Too?

Do to others what you want them
to do to you.

Matthew 7:12 NCV

Would you like to make the world a better place? If so, you can start by being a girlfriend who practices the Golden Rule.

Some rules are easier *to understand* than they are *to live by*, and the Golden Rule certainly fits that description. Jesus told us that we should treat other people in the same way that we would want to be treated. But sometimes, especially when we're tired, upset, jealous, or insecure, that rule is very hard to follow.

Jesus wants us to treat other people with respect, kindness, courtesy, and love. When we do, we make our families and friends happy . . . and we make our Father in heaven very proud.

So if you're wondering how to make the world a better place, here's a great place to start: let the Golden Rule be your rule, too. And if you want to know how to treat other people, ask the girl you see every time you look into the mirror. The answer you receive *from her* will tell you exactly what to do.

The Golden Rule starts at home,
but it should never stop there.

Marie T. Freeman

I have discovered that when I please Christ,
I end up inadvertently serving others
far more effectively.

Beth Moore

In the very place where God has put us,
whatever its limitations,
whatever kind of work it may be,
we may indeed serve the Lord Christ.

Elisabeth Elliot

Thought for the Day

How Would *You* Feel?

When you're trying to decide how to treat
another person, ask yourself this question:
"How would I feel if somebody treated me
that way?" Then, treat the other person
the way that you would want
to be treated.

More Words from God's Word

*And be careful that when you get
on each other's nerves you don't snap
at each other. Look for the best in each other,
and always do your best to bring it out.*

1 Thessalonians 5:15 MSG

*Don't be obsessed with getting your own
advantage. Forget yourselves long enough
to lend a helping hand.*

Philippians 2:4 MSG

Now I Pray

Dear Lord, let me treat others as I wish
to be treated. Because I expect kindness,
let me be kind. Because I wish to be loved,
let me be loving. Because I need forgiveness,
let me be merciful. In all things, Lord,
let me live by the Golden Rule that is
the commandment of Your Son Jesus.

Amen

Chapter 6

When People Aren't Nice

Do not fret because of evildoers;
don't envy the wicked.

Proverbs 24:19 NLT

Face it: sometimes people can be cruel . . . very cruel. When other people are unkind to you or to your friends, you may be tempted to strike back, either verbally or in some other way. Don't do it! Instead, remember that God corrects other people's behaviors in His own way, and He doesn't need your help (even if you're totally convinced that He does!). Remember that God has commanded you to forgive others, just as you, too, must sometimes seek forgiveness from others.

So, when other people behave cruelly, foolishly, or impulsively—as they will from time to time—don't be a hotheaded girl. Instead, speak up for yourself as politely as you can, and walk away. Then, forgive everybody as quickly as you can, and leave the rest up to God.

You don't have to attend
every argument you're invited to!

Anonymous

Beware of over-great pleasure in being
popular or even beloved.

Margaret Fuller

If you just set out to be liked, you would be
prepared to compromise on anything
at anytime, and you would achieve nothing.

Margaret Thatcher

Thought for the Day

Stand Up for What's Right!

If one of your friends is being cruel, unkind,
or discourteous, don't join in! Instead, stand up
for the people who need your help.
Remember what Jesus said:
when you help people in need,
you're helping Him, too
(Matthew 25:40).

More Words from God's Word

Hatred stirs up trouble,
but love forgives all wrongs.

Proverbs 10:12 NCV

You have heard it said,
"Love your neighbor and hate your enemy."
But I tell you: Love your enemies and
pray for those who persecute you,
that you may be sons of your Father in heaven.

Matthew 5:43-45 NIV

Now I Pray

Lord, You have given me love that is beyond
human understanding, and I am Your loving
servant. Let the love that I feel for You be
reflected in the compassion that I show
to my family, to my friends,
and to everybody I meet.
Amen

Chapter 7

The Power of Faith

*But Jesus turned him about, and when he saw her,
he said, Daughter, be of good comfort;
thy faith hath made thee whole.
And the woman was made whole
from that hour.*

Matthew 9:22 KJV

every life—including yours—is a series of successes and failures, celebrations and disappointments, joys and sorrows. Every step of the way, through every triumph and tragedy, God will stand by your side and strengthen you . . . *if* you have faith in Him. Jesus taught His disciples that if they had faith, they could move mountains. You can too.

When a suffering woman sought healing by merely touching the hem of His cloak, Jesus replied, "thy faith hath made thee whole." The message to believers of every generation is clear: we must live by faith today and every day.

It's a fact: when you place your faith, your trust, indeed your life, in the hands of Christ Jesus, you'll be amazed at the marvelous things He can do with you and through you. So strengthen your faith through praise, through worship, through Bible study, and through prayer. And trust God's plans. With Him, all things are possible, and He stands ready to open a world of possibilities to you . . . *if* you have faith.

Faith in faith is pointless.
Faith in a living, active God moves mountains.

Beth Moore

Faith is nothing more or less
than actively trusting God.

Catherine Marshall

Jesus taught that the evidence that confirms
our leaps of faith comes after we risk believing,
not before.

Gloria Gaither

Thought for the Day

Don't Be Embarrassed
to Discuss Your Faith:

You don't have to attend seminary
to have worthwhile opinions about your faith,
so don't be afraid to share your testimony.

More Words from God's Word

So, you see, it is impossible to please God without faith. Anyone who wants to come to him must believe that there is a God and that he rewards those who sincerely seek him.

Hebrews 11:6 NLT

Everything is possible
to the one who believes.

Mark 9:23 HCSB

Now I Pray

Dear Lord, in the dark moments of my life,
help me to remember that You are always near
and that You can overcome any challenge.
Keep me mindful of Your love and Your power,
so that I may live courageously and
faithfully today and every day.
Amen

Chapter 8

The Journey toward Spiritual Maturity

*Grow in grace and understanding
of our Master and Savior, Jesus Christ.
Glory to the Master,
now and forever! Yes!*

2 Peter 3:18 MSG

When will you be a "fully-grown" Christian woman? Hopefully never—or at least not until you arrive in heaven! As a believer living here on planet Earth, you're never "fully grown"; you always have the potential to keep growing.

In those quiet moments when you open your heart to God, the One who made you *keeps* remaking you. He gives you direction, perspective, wisdom, and courage.

Would you like a time-tested formula for spiritual growth? Here it is: Keep studying God's Word, keep obeying His commandments, keep praying (and listening for answers), and keep trying to live in the center of God's will. When you do, you'll never stay stuck for long. You will, instead, be a growing Christian . . . and that's precisely the kind of Christian God wants you, and everyone else, to be.

Growing in any area of the Christian life
takes time, and the key is daily
sitting at the feet of Jesus.
Cynthia Heald

The Christian gives all she knows of herself to all
she knows of God and continues to grow
in the knowledge of both.
Gladys Hunt

I do not know how the Spirit of Christ performs it,
but He brings us choices through which
we constantly change, fresh and new,
into His likeness.
Joni Eareckson Tada

Thought for the Day

How Do I Know if I Can
Still Keep Growing as a Christian?
Check your pulse.
If it's still beating,
then you can still keep growing.

More Words from God's Word

When I was a child, I spoke and thought
and reasoned as a child does.
But when I grew up, I put away childish things.

1 Corinthians 13:11 NLT

There has never been the slightest doubt in
my mind that the God who started this great work
in you would keep at it and bring it to
a flourishing finish on the very day
Christ Jesus appears.

Philippians 1:6 MSG

Now I Pray

Dear Lord, the Bible tells me that You are
at work in my life, continuing to help me grow
and to mature in my faith. Show me
Your wisdom, Father, and let me live
according to Your Word and Your will.
Amen

Chapter 9

About to Make a Big Decision?

Pray about It!

When a believing person prays,
great things happen.

James 5:16 NCV

RADICAL DEVOTIONS

On his second missionary journey, Paul started a small church in Thessalonica. A short time later, he penned a letter that was intended to encourage the new believers at that church. Today, almost 2,000 years later, 1 Thessalonians remains a powerful, practical guide for Christian living.

In his letter, Paul advised members of the new church to "pray without ceasing." His advice applies to Christians of every generation. When we consult God on an hourly basis, we receive His wisdom, His strength, and His guidance. And, as Corrie ten Boom observed, "Any concern that is too small to be turned into a prayer is too small to be made into a burden."

Today, instead of turning things over in your mind, turn them over to God in prayer. Instead of worrying about your next decision, ask God to lead the way. Don't limit your prayers to meals or bedtime. Transform yourself into a woman of constant prayer. God is listening, and He wants to hear from you. Now.

About to Make a Big Decision? Pray about It!

We must leave it to God to answer
our prayers in His own wisest way. Sometimes,
we are so impatient and think that God does not
answer. God always answers! He never fails!
Be still. Abide in Him.

Mrs. Charles E. Cowman

As we join together in prayer,
we draw on God's enabling might in a way that
multiplies our own efforts many times over.

Shirley Dobson

Don't be overwhelmed . . .
take it one day and one prayer at a time.

Stormie Omartian

Thought for the Day

Pray Early and Often:

One way to make sure that your heart
is in tune with God is to pray often.
The more you talk to God,
the more He will talk to you.

More Words from God's Word

One day Jesus told his disciples a story
to illustrate their need for constant prayer
and to show them that they must never give up.

Luke 18:1 NLT

Don't fret or worry. Instead of worrying, pray.
Let petitions and praises shape your worries
into prayers, letting God know your concerns.
Before you know it, a sense of God's wholeness,
everything coming together for good,
will come and settle you down. It's wonderful
what happens when Christ displaces worry
at the center of your life.

Philippians 4:6-7 MSG

Now I Pray

I pray to You, Dear Lord, because You desire it
and because I need it. Prayer not only changes
things, it changes me. Help me, Lord,
never to face the challenges of the day
without first spending time with You.

Amen

Chapter 10

Can They Tell You're a Christian?

*Be an example to the believers in word,
in conduct, in love, in spirit,
in faith, in purity.*

1 Timothy 4:12 NKJV

RADICAL DEVOTIONS

Whether we like it or not, all of us are role models. Our friends and family members watch our actions and, as followers of Christ, we are obliged to act accordingly.

What kind of example are you? Are you a woman whose behavior serves as a positive role model for others? Are you the kind of person whose actions, day in and day out, are based upon kindness, faithfulness, and a love for the Lord? If so, you are not only blessed by God, you are also a powerful force for good in a world that desperately needs positive influences such as yours.

We live in a dangerous, temptation-filled world. That's why you encounter so many opportunities to stray from God's commandments. Resist those temptations! When you do, you'll earn God's blessings *and* you'll serve as positive role model for your family and friends.

Corrie ten Boom advised, "Don't worry about what you do not understand. Worry about what you do understand in the Bible but do not live by." And that's sound advice because our families and friends are watching . . . and so, for that matter, is God.

The religion of Jesus Christ
has an ethical as well as a doctrinal side.

Lottie Moon

Our souls were made to live in
an upper atmosphere, and we stifle and
choke if we live on any lower level.
Our eyes were made to look off from
these heavenly heights, and our vision
is distorted by any lower gazing.

Hannah Whitall Smith

Thought for the Day

Your Life Is a Sermon:
preach and teach accordingly:
The sermons you live are far more
important than the ones you give.

More Words from God's Word

*I have set you an example that you should
do as I have done for you.*

John 13:15 NIV

*In every way be an example of doing
good deeds. When you teach,
do it with honesty and seriousness.*

Titus 2:7 NCV

*You are the light that gives light to the world.
In the same way, you should be a light for other
people. Live so that they will see the good things
you do and will praise your Father in heaven.*

Matthew 5:14, 16 NCV

Now I Pray

Lord, make me a good example to my family
and friends. Let the things that I say
and do show everybody what it means
to be a good person and a good christian.
Amen

Chapter 11

Give Me Patience, Lord, and Give It to Me Now!

Patience is better than pride.

Ecclesiastes 7:8 NLT

The dictionary defines the word *patience* as "the ability to be calm, tolerant, and understanding." If that describes you, you can skip the rest of this page. But, if you're like most of us, you'd better keep reading.

For most of us, patience is a hard thing to master. Why? Because we have lots of things we want, and we want them NOW . . . if not sooner. But the Bible tells us that we must learn to wait patiently for the things that God has in store for our lives.

The next time you find your patience tested to the limit, remember that the world unfolds according to God's timetable, not yours. Sometimes, you must wait patiently, and that's as it should be. After all, think how patient God has been with you!

Let me encourage you to continue
to wait with faith. God may not perform
a miracle, but He is trustworthy to touch you
and make you whole
where there used to be a hole.

Lisa Whelchel

Patience means waiting for God faithfully,
hopefully, and prayerfully.
But patience also means being willing
to accept God's timetable, not our own.

Marie T. Freeman

Thought for the Day

Patience Is . . .
a virtue that carries a lot of wait.

More Words from God's Word

Be joyful because you have hope.
Be patient when trouble comes,
and pray at all times.

Romans 12:12 NCV

I wait quietly before God, for my salvation
comes from him. He alone is my rock
and my salvation,
my fortress where I will never be shaken.

Psalm 62:1-2 NLT

Now I Pray

Lord, sometimes I am not very patient.
Slow me down and calm me down.
Help me to think wisely and to act wisely.
Today and every day, help me to learn
the wisdom of patience.

Amen

Chapter 12

When the Questions Outnumber the Answers

When doubts filled my mind,
your comfort gave me
renewed hope and cheer.

Psalm 94:19 NLT

Have you ever felt your faith in God slipping away? If so, you are not alone. Even the most faithful Christians are overcome by occasional bouts of fear and doubt, and so, too, will you.

Doubts come in several shapes and sizes: doubts about God, doubts about the future, and doubts about our own abilities, for starters. And what, precisely, does God's Word say in response to these doubts? The Bible is clear: when we are beset by doubts, of whatever kind, we must draw ourselves nearer to God through worship and through prayer. When we do so, God, the loving Father who has never left our sides, draws ever closer to us (James 4:8).

Will your faith be tested from time to time? Of course it will be. And will you have doubts about God's willingness to fulfill His promises? Perhaps you will. But even when you feel far removed from God, God never leaves your side, not for an instant. He is always with you, always willing to calm the storms of life. When you sincerely seek His presence—and when you genuinely seek to establish a deeper, more meaningful relationship with His Son—God is prepared to touch your heart, to calm your fears, to answer your doubts, and to restore your soul.

Ignoring Him by neglecting prayer and Bible reading will cause you to doubt.

Anne Graham Lotz

If you feed your faith, your doubts will starve to death.

Anonymous

Thought for the Day

When In Doubt . . . Talk It Out!
If you're uncertain about a particular situation or if you have doubts about your faith, talk it over with somebody you trust.

More Words from God's Word

I tell you the truth, if you have faith and
do not doubt . . . you can say to this mountain
"Go and throw yourself into the sea,"
and it will be done.

Matthew 21:21 NIV

But he must ask in faith without any doubting,
for the one who doubts is like the surf of the sea,
driven and tossed by the wind.

James 1:6 NASB

Now I Pray

Dear God, sometimes this world can be
a puzzling place. When I am unsure of
my next step, keep me aware that You
are always near. Give me faith, Father,
and let me remember that with Your love
and Your power, I can live courageously
and faithfully today and every day.

Amen

Chapter 13

Sharing Your Faith

*All those who stand before others
and say they believe in me,
I will say before my Father in heaven
that they belong to me.*

Matthew 10:32 NCV

RADICAL DEVOTIONS

Let's face the facts: those of us who are Christians should be willing to talk about the things that Christ has done for us. Our personal testimonies are vitally important, but sometimes, because of shyness or insecurities, we're afraid to share our experiences. And that's unfortunate.

In his second letter to Timothy, Paul shares a message to believers of every generation when he writes, "God has not given us a spirit of timidity" (1:7). Paul's meaning is crystal clear: When sharing our testimonies, we must be courageous and unashamed.

We live in a world that desperately needs the healing message of Christ Jesus. Every believer, each in his or her own way, bears responsibility for sharing the Good News of our Savior. And it is important to remember that we bear testimony through both words and actions.

If you seek to be a radical follower of Christ, then it's time for you to share your testimony with others. So today, preach the Gospel through your words and your deeds . . . but not necessarily in that order.

There are many timid souls whom
we jostle morning and evening as we pass
them by; but if only the kind word were spoken
they might become fully persuaded.

Fanny Crosby

Theology is an interesting school of thought.
The Bible is beautiful literature. Sitting in quiet
sanctuary, bathed in the amber light from
stained-glass windows, having our jangled nerves
soothed by the chords from an organ—all that is
inspiring. But to tell you the truth, when we leave
the classroom, close the church door, and walk
out into the real world, it is the indisputable proof
of changed lives that makes us believers.

Gloria Gaither

Thought for the Day

What If I'm Uncomfortable Talking about My Faith?

Remember: you're not giving the State of
the Union Address—you're having
a conversation. And besides, if you're not sure
what to say, a good place to start is by
asking questions, not making speeches.

More Words from God's Word

Be wise in the way you act with people
who are not believers,
making the most of every opportunity.

Colossians 4:5 NCV

For God has not given us a spirit of fear and
timidity, but of power, love, and self-discipline.
So you must never be ashamed
to tell others about our Lord.

2 Timothy 1:7-8 NLT

Now I Pray

Dear Lord, You have offered me the gift of
eternal life through the gift of Your Son
Jesus. Let me share the story of my salvation
with others so that they, too,
might dedicate their lives to Christ
and receive His eternal gifts.

Amen

Chapter 14

Looking for God's Plan . . . and Trusting It

"I say this because I know what I am planning for you," says the Lord. "I have good plans for you, not plans to hurt you. I will give you hope and a good future."

Jeremiah 29:11 NCV

God is good, and God is in charge—even when bad things happen. Sometimes, of course, we don't know why things happen as they do. But God does. Yet, the knowledge that God knows exactly what He is doing may offer us very little comfort. Often, we become discouraged, or worse. When loved ones are taken from us, we cry bitter tears. When we witness the pain of people here at home or the pain of people far away, we wonder why. Sometimes, despite our prayers and our tears, our questions must go unanswered—for now.

Thankfully, there will come a day when our sadness will vanish and our questions will be answered. But until then, we will, on occasion, weep tears of sadness when bad things happen. Why? Because we simply can't understand all the reasons that our world unfolds as it does. Yet God understands, and He has the final word.

God doesn't answer all of our questions, but He does expect us to do something about them. When we wonder why the world isn't a better place, God expects to answer that question with willing hands and heartfelt prayers.

When we accept God's love and His Son, we receive the Answer (with a capital A) to the troubles of our world. It's precisely that Answer that gives us the hope, the courage, and the faith to trust our Heavenly Father today, tomorrow, and forever.

The only thing that can hinder us is our own failure to work in harmony with the plans of the Creator, and if this lack of harmony can be removed, then God can work.

Hannah Whitall Smith

Thought for the Day

Big, Bigger, and Very Big Plans:
God has very big plans in store for your life, so trust Him and wait patiently for those plans to unfold. And remember:
God's timing is best.

More Words from God's Word

For God is working in you,
giving you the desire to obey him
and the power to do what pleases him.

Philippians 2:13 NLT

The LORD will work out his plans for my life—
for your faithful love, O LORD, endures forever.

Psalm 138:8 NLT

Now I Pray

Dear Lord, I am Your creation, and You created
me for a reason. Give me the wisdom to follow
Your direction for my life's journey.
Let me do Your work here on earth by seeking
Your will and living it, knowing that when
I trust in You, Father, I am eternally blessed.
Amen

Chapter 15

Friendships That Are Pleasing to God

As iron sharpens iron,
a friend sharpens a friend.

Proverbs 27:17 NLT

Because we tend to become like our friends, we must choose our friends carefully. Because our friends influence us in ways that are both subtle and powerful, we must ensure that our friendships honor God. Because our friends have the power to lift us up or to bring us down, we must select friends who, by their words and their actions, encourage us to lead Christ-centered lives.

When we build lasting friendships that are pleasing to God, we are blessed. When we seek out encouraging friends and mentors, they lift us up. And, when we make ourselves a powerful source of encouragement to others, we do God's work here on earth.

Do you seek to be a godly Christian woman? If so, you should build friendships that honor your Creator. When you do, God will bless you and your friends, today and forever.

In friendship, God opens your eyes
to the glories of Himself.

Joni Eareckson Tada

Friends are angels who lift our feet
when our own wings have trouble
remembering how to fly.

Anonymous

Thought for the Day

The Best Rule for Making Friends . . .
is the Golden one.

More Words from God's Word

A friend loves at all times.

Proverbs 17:17 NIV

*Greater love has no one than this,
that he lay down his life for his friends.*

John 15:13 NIV

Now I Pray

Lord, thank You for my friends.
Let me be a trustworthy friend to others,
and let my love for You be reflected in
my genuine love for them.
Amen

Chapter 16

Pleasing Whom?

Do you think I am trying to make people
accept me? No, God is the One I am trying
to please. Am I trying to please people?
If I still wanted to please people,
I would not be a servant of Christ.

Galatians 1:10 NCV

Sometimes, it's very tempting to be a people-pleaser. But usually, it's the wrong thing to do.

When we worry too much about pleasing our friends, we may not worry enough about pleasing God—and when we fail to please God, we inevitably pay a very high price for our mistaken priorities.

Whom will you try to please today: God or your friends? Your obligation is most certainly *not* to imperfect guys or girls. Your obligation is to an all-knowing and perfect God. Trust Him always. Love Him always. Praise Him always. And seek to please Him and *only* Him. Always.

It is comfortable to know that we
are responsible to God and not to man.
It is a small matter to be judged
of man's judgement.

Lottie Moon

When we are set free from the bondage
of pleasing others, when we are free from
currying others' favor and others' approval—
then no one will be able to make us
miserable or dissatisfied. And then,
if we know we have pleased God,
contentment will be our consolation.

Kay Arthur

You will get untold flak for prioritizing
God's revealed and present will for your life
over man's . . . but, boy, is it worth it.

Beth Moore

Thought for the Day

**Remember that it's more important
to be respected than to be liked**.

More Words from God's Word

*Our only goal is to please God whether
we live here or there, because we must
all stand before Christ to be judged.*

2 Corinthians 5:9-10 NCV

*Whoever walks with the wise will become wise;
whoever walks with fools will suffer harm.*

Proverbs 13:20 NLT

Now I Pray

Dear Lord, today I will worry less about
pleasing other people and more about
pleasing You. I will honor You with my thoughts,
my actions, and my prayers. And I will worship
You, Father, with thanksgiving in my heart,
this day and forever.

Amen

Chapter 17

Becoming an Optimistic Believer

But we are hoping for something
we do not have yet,
and we are waiting for it patiently.

Romans 8:25 NCV

are you a *radically* optimistic believer? Do you believe that God has a wonderful plan that is perfectly suited for your life? And do you believe that when your life here on earth is done, you will enjoy the priceless gift of eternal life? Hopefully so, because Christianity and pessimism don't mix. Why? Because Christians have every reason to be optimistic about life here on earth *and* life eternal.

Mrs. Charles E. Cowman advised, "Never yield to gloomy anticipation. Place your hope and confidence in God. He has no record of failure." But sometimes, despite our trust in God, we may fall into the spiritual traps of worry, frustration, or sheer exhaustion, and our hearts become heavy. What's needed is plenty of rest, a large dose of perspective, and plenty of prayer, but not necessarily in that order.

Today, make this promise to yourself and keep it: vow to be a hope-filled Christian. Think optimistically about your life *and* your future. Trust your hopes, not your fears. Take time to celebrate God's glorious creation. And then, when you've filled your heart with hope and gladness, share your optimism with your friends. They'll be better for it, and so will you. But not necessarily in that order.

If you can't tell whether your glass is half-empty or half-full, you don't need another glass; what you need is better eyesight . . . and a more thankful heart.

Marie T. Freeman

Thought for the Day

Be a Realistic Optimist:

Your attitude toward the future will help create your future. So think realistically about yourself and your situation while making a conscious effort to focus on hopes, not fears. When you do, you'll put the self-fulfilling prophecy to work for you.

More Words from God's Word

*I can do everything through him
that gives me strength.*

Philippians 4:13 NIV

*For God has not given us a spirit of fear,
but of power and of love and of a sound mind.*

2 Timothy 1:7 NLT

*Wisdom is pleasing to you.
If you find it, you have hope for the future.*

Proverbs 24:14 NCV

Now I Pray

Lord, give me faith, optimism, and hope.
Let me expect the best from You,
and let me look for the best in others.
Let me trust You, Lord, to direct my life.
And, let me be Your faithful, hopeful,
optimistic servant every day that I live.

Amen

Chapter 18

Stuff, Stuff, and More Stuff

Yes, a person is a fool to store up
earthly wealth but not have
a rich relationship with God.

Luke 12:21 NLT

"**S**o much stuff to shop for, and so little time . . ." These words seem to describe the priorities of our 21st-century world. Hopefully, you're not building your life around your next visit to the local mall—but you can be sure that many people are!

Our society is in love with money and the things that money can buy. God is not. God cares about people, not possessions, and so must we. We must, to the best of our abilities, love our neighbors as ourselves, and we must, to the best of our abilities, resist the mighty temptation to place possessions ahead of people.

Money, in and of itself, is not evil; worshipping money is. So today, as you prioritize matters of importance for you and yours, remember that God is almighty, but the dollar is not. If we worship God, we are blessed. But if we worship "the almighty dollar," we are inevitably punished because of our misplaced priorities—and our punishment inevitably comes sooner rather than later.

I have held many things in my hands,
and I have lost them all;
but whatever I have placed in God's hands,
that I still possess.

Corrie ten Boom

It's sobering to contemplate how much time,
effort, sacrifice, compromise,
and attention we give to acquiring
and increasing our supply of something
that is totally insignificant in eternity.

Anne Graham Lotz

Why is love of gold more potent
than love of souls?

Lottie Moon

Thought for the Day

Stuff 101:
The world says, "Buy more stuff."
God says, "Stuff isn't important."
Believe God.

More Words from God's Word

No one can serve two masters.
The person will hate one master and
love the other, or will follow one master
and refuse to follow the other.
You cannot serve both God and worldly riches.

Matthew 6:24 NCV

Then Jesus said to them,
"Be careful and guard against all kinds of greed.
Life is not measured by how much one owns."

Luke 12:15 NCV

Now I Pray

Lord, my greatest possession is my relationship
with You through Jesus Christ. You have
promised that, when I first seek
Your kingdom and Your righteousness, You will
give me whatever I need. Let me trust
You completely, Lord, for my needs, both
material and spiritual, this day and always.

Amen

Chapter 19

Peer Pressure 101

*Our only goal is to please God
whether we live here or there,
because we must all
stand before Christ to be judged.*

2 Corinthians 5:9-10 NCV

Rick Warren observed, "Those who follow the crowd usually get lost in it." We know those words to be true, but oftentimes we fail to live by them. Instead of trusting God for guidance, we imitate our friends and suffer the consequences. Instead of seeking to please our Father in heaven, we strive to please our peers, with decidedly mixed results. Instead of doing the right thing, we do the "easy" thing or the "popular" thing. And when we do, we pay a high price for our shortsightedness.

Would you like a time-tested formula for successful living? Here is a simple formula that is proven and true: don't give in to peer pressure. Period.

Instead of getting lost in the crowd, you should find guidance from God. Does this sound too simple? Perhaps it *is* simple, but it is also the only way to reap all the marvelous riches that God has in store for you.

For better or worse, you will eventually become
more and more like the people you
associate with. So why not associate with
people who make you better, not worse?

Marie T. Freeman

Make God's will the focus of your life day by day.
If you seek to please Him and Him alone,
you'll find yourself satisfied with life.

Kay Arthur

Get ready for God to show you not only
His pleasure, but His approval.

Joni Eareckson Tada

Thought for the Day

**If You Try to Please
All the People, You Lose.**
If you try to please God, you win.

More Words from God's Word

*Do you think I am trying to make people
accept me? No, God is the One I am trying
to please. Am I trying to please people?
If I still wanted to please people,
I would not be a servant of Christ.*

Galatians 1:10 NCV

*It is impossible to please God apart from faith.
And why? Because anyone who wants
to approach God must believe both
that he exists and that he cares enough to
respond to those who seek him.*

Hebrews 1:6 MSG

Now I Pray

Dear Lord, today I will honor You.
I will seek to please You with my thoughts
and my actions as I strive to be
a faithful servant to your son.
Amen

Chapter 20

An Attitude of Gratitude

Be cheerful no matter what; pray all the time;
thank God no matter what happens.
This is the way God wants you
who belong to Christ Jesus to live.

1 Thessalonians 5:16-18 MSG

if you're like most females on the planet, you're a *very* busy girl. Your life is probably hectic, demanding, and complicated. When the demands of life leave you rushing from place to place with scarcely a moment to spare, you may fail to pause and thank your Creator for the blessings He has bestowed upon you. Big mistake.

No matter how busy you are, you should never be too busy to thank God for His gifts. Your task, as a radical believer in a living Christ, is to praise God many times each day. Then, with gratitude in your heart, you can face your daily duties with the perspective and power that only He can provide.

If you won't fill your heart with gratitude,
the devil will fill it with something else.

Marie T. Freeman

If you pause to think—
you'll have cause to thank!

Anonymous

Thought for the Day

When Is the Best Time to Say "Thanks" to God?

When you're inhaling,
or when you're exhaling,
or in between.

Face facts: you live in a temptation-filled world. The devil is hard at work in your neighborhood, and so are his helpers. Here in the 21st century, the bad guys are working around the clock to lead you astray. That's why you must remain vigilant.

In a letter to believers, Peter offers a stern warning: "Your adversary, the devil, prowls around like a roaring lion, seeking someone to devour" (I Peter 5:8 NASB). What was true in New Testament times is equally true in our own. Satan tempts his prey and then devours them (and it's up to you—and only you—to make sure that you're not one of the ones being devoured!).

As a believer who seeks a radical relationship with Jesus, you must beware because temptations are everywhere. Satan is determined to win; you must be equally determined that he does not.

Because Christ has faced our every temptation
without sin, we never face a temptation
that has no door of escape.

Beth Moore

As a child of God,
you are no longer a slave to sin.

Kay Arthur

Thought for the Day

We Live in a Temptation Generation:
You can find temptation in lots of places.
Your job is to avoid those places!

More Words from God's Word

Watch and pray so that you will not fall
into temptation. The spirit is willing
but the body is weak.

Matthew 26:41 NIV

Then Jesus told him, "Go away, Satan!
For it is written: You must worship the Lord
your God, and you must serve Him only."

Matthew 4:10 HCSB

Now I Pray

Dear Lord, help me to behave myself like
a faithful follower of Your son. Let me keep
christ in my heart, and let me put
the devil in his place: far away from me!
Amen

Chapter 22

The Power of Words

*May the words of my mouth and the thoughts
of my heart be pleasing to you,
O LORD, my rock and my redeemer.*

Psalm 19:14 NLT

The words that we speak have great power. If our words are encouraging, we can lift others up; if our words are hurtful, we can hold others back. The Bible reminds us that "Reckless words pierce like a sword, but the tongue of the wise brings healing" (Proverbs 12:18 NIV). In other words, if we are to solve more problems than we start, we must measure our words carefully.

Sometimes, even the most thoughtful girlfriends may speak first and think second (with decidedly mixed results). A far better strategy, of course, is to do the more difficult thing: to think first and to speak next.

Do you seek to be a source of encouragement to others? And, do you seek to be a worthy ambassador for Christ? If so, you must speak words that are worthy of your Savior. So avoid angry outbursts. Refrain from impulsive outpourings. Terminate tantrums. Instead, speak words of encouragement and hope to a world that desperately needs both.

The things that we feel most deeply
we ought to learn to be silent about,
at least until we have talked them over
thoroughly with God.

Elisabeth Elliot

A little kindly advice is better than
a great deal of scolding.

Fanny Crosby

Thought for the Day

Think First, Speak Second:
If you want to keep from hurting
other people's feelings,
don't open your mouth
until you've turned on your brain.

More Words from God's Word

Kind words are like honey—
sweet to the soul and healthy for the body.

Proverbs 16:24 NLT

Watch the way you talk.
Let nothing foul or dirty come out of your mouth.
Say only what helps, each word a gift.

Ephesians 4:29 MSG

Now I Pray

Dear Lord, make my words pleasing to You.
Let me be a source of encouragement
to others as I share a message of faith
and assurance with the world.
Today, I will honor You, Father,
by choosing my words carefully,
thoughtfully, and lovingly.
Amen

Chapter 23

Choices That Are Pleasing to God

*I have set before you life and death,
blessings and curses. Now choose life, so that
you and your children may live and that you
may love the LORD your God, listen to his voice,
and hold fast to him.*

Deuteronomy 30:19-20 NIV

Life is a series of choices. From the instant we wake in the morning until the moment we nod off to sleep at night, we make countless decisions: decisions about the things we do, decisions about the words we speak, and decisions about the thoughts we choose to think. Simply put, the quality of those decisions determines the quality of our lives.

As radical believers who have been saved by a loving and merciful God, we have every reason to make wise choices. Yet sometimes, amid the inevitable hustle and bustle of life here on earth, we allow ourselves to behave in ways that we know are displeasing to God. When we do, we forfeit—albeit temporarily—the joy and the peace that we might otherwise experience through Him.

As you consider the next step in your life's journey, take time to consider how many things in this life you can control: your thoughts, your words, your priorities, and your actions, for starters. And then, if you sincerely want to discover God's purpose for your life, make choices that are pleasing to Him. He deserves no less . . . and neither do you.

God is voting for us all the time.
The devil is voting against us all the time.
The way we vote carries the election.

Corrie ten Boom

There may be no trumpet sound or
loud applause when we make a right decision,
just a calm sense of resolution and peace.

Gloria Gaither

I do not know how the Spirit of Christ performs
it, but He brings us choices through which we
constantly change, fresh and new,
into His likeness.

Joni Eareckson Tada

Thought for the Day

Slow Down! If you're about to make
an important choice, don't be impulsive.
Remember: big decisions have big
consequences, and if you don't think
about those consequences now,
you may pay a big price later.

More Words from God's Word

Therefore, get your minds ready for action,
being self-disciplined, and set your hope
completely on the grace to be brought to you
at the revelation of Jesus Christ. As obedient
children, do not be conformed to the desires
of your former ignorance but, as the One who
called you is holy, you also are to be holy
in all your conduct.

1 Peter 1:13-15 HCSB

Jesus answered, "If people love me, they will
obey my teaching. My Father will love them,
and we will come to them
and make our home with them."

John 14:23 NCV

Now I Pray

Lord, help me to make choices that are pleasing
to You. Help me to be honest, patient, and kind.
And above all, help me to follow the teachings
of Jesus, not just today, but every day.

Amen

Chapter 24

Whose Priorities?

The thing you should want most is God's kingdom
and doing what God wants.
Then all these other things you need
will be given to you.

Matthew 6:33 NCV

Who is in charge of your heart? Is it God, or is it something else? Have you given Christ your heart, your soul, your talents, your time, and your testimony? Or are you giving Him little more than a few hours each Sunday morning?

In the book of Exodus, God warns that we should place no gods before Him. Yet all too often, we place our Lord in second, third, or fourth place as we worship other things. When we unwittingly place possessions or relationships above our love for the Creator, we create big problems for ourselves.

Does God rule your heart? Make certain that the honest answer to this question is a resounding yes. In the life of every radical believer, God comes first. And that's precisely the place that He deserves in *your* heart.

Jesus challenges you and me to keep
our focus daily on the cross of His will
if we want to be His disciples.

Anne Graham Lotz

Have you prayed about your resources lately?
Find out how God wants you to use your time
and your money. No matter what it costs,
forsake all that is not of God.

Kay Arthur

The manifold rewards of a serious, consistent
prayer life demonstrate clearly that time with
our Lord should be our first priority.

Shirley Dobson

Thought for the Day

**Unless You Put First Things First,
You're Bound to Finish Last:**
And don't forget that putting first things first
means God first.

More Words from God's Word

Let us fix our eyes on Jesus, the author and perfecter of our faith, who for the joy set before him endured the cross, scorning its shame, and sat down at the right hand of the throne of God.

Hebrews 12:2 NIV

He said to them all, "If anyone desires to come after Me, let him deny himself, and take up his cross daily, and follow Me. For whoever desires to save his life will lose it, but whoever loses his life for My sake will save it.

Luke 9:23-24 NKJV

Now I Pray

Lord, let Your priorities be my priorities. Let Your will be my will. Let Your Word be my guide, and let me grow in faith and in wisdom this day and every day.

Amen

Chapter 25

Searching for Mr. Right
(While Avoiding Mr. Wrong)

*Now these three remain: faith, hope, and love.
But the greatest of these is love.*

1 Corinthians 13:13 HCSB

More Words from God's Word

*Do not be unequally yoked together
with unbelievers. For what fellowship has
righteousness with lawlessness?
And what communion has light with darkness?*

2 Corinthians 6:14 NKJV

*Let love and faithfulness never leave you . . .
write them on the tablet of your heart.*

Proverbs 3:3 NIV

*Charm is deceptive, and beauty is fleeting;
but a woman who fears the LORD is to be praised.*

Proverbs 31:30 NIV

Now I Pray

Dear Lord, You have brought family members
and friends into my life. Let me love them,
let me help them, let me treasure them,
and let me lead them to You.

Amen

Chapter 26

Forgiveness Starts in the Mirror

*Blessed are those who
do not condemn themselves.*

Romans 14:22 NLT

Being patient with other people can be difficult. But sometimes, we find it even more difficult to be patient with ourselves. We have high expectations and lofty goals. We want to receive God's blessings now, not later. And, of course, we want our lives to unfold according to our own wishes and our own timetables—not God's. Yet throughout the Bible, we are instructed that patience is the companion of wisdom. Proverbs 16:32 teaches us that "Patience is better than strength" (NCV). God's message, then, is clear: we must be patient with all people, beginning with that particular girl who stares back at us each time we gaze into the mirror.

Faith in God leads to self-acceptance. Without God, a girl may be plagued with doubts about self-worth and self-esteem. But, the thoughtful believer knows that God created her in His image and that she was recreated by her belief in God's Son.

The Bible affirms the importance of self-acceptance by exhorting believers to love others as they love themselves (Matthew 22:37-40). Furthermore, the Bible teaches that when we genuinely open our hearts to Him, God accepts us just as we are. And, if He accepts us—faults and all—then who are we to believe otherwise?

Your self worth is more important
than your net worth.

Anonymous

As you and I lay up for ourselves living,
lasting treasures in Heaven,
we come to the awesome conclusion
that we ourselves are His treasure!

Anne Graham Lotz

Thought for the Day

Don't Worry Too Much about Self-esteem:
Instead, worry more about living a life that is pleasing to God. Learn to think optimistically. Find a worthy purpose. Find people to love and people to serve. When you do, your self-esteem will, on most days, take care of itself.

More Words from God's Word

For you made us only a little lower than God,
and you crowned us with glory and honor.

Psalm 8:5 NLT

As the Father loved Me, I also have loved you;
abide in My love.

John 15:9 NKJV

Now I Pray

Lord, I have so much to learn and so many ways
to improve myself, but You love me just as I am.
Thank You for Your love and for Your Son.
And, help me to become the person
that You want me to become.

Amen

Chapter 27

Are You Listening, God?

"For I know the plans I have for you,"
declares the Lord, "plans to prosper you and not
to harm you, plans to give you hope and a future.
Then you will call upon me and come and
pray to me, and I will listen to you."

Jeremiah 29:11-12 NIV

*i*n case you've been wondering, wonder no more—God *does* answer your prayers. What God *does not* do is this: He does not always answer your prayers as soon as you might like, and He does not always answer your prayers by saying "Yes."

God isn't an order-taker, and He's not some sort of cosmic vending machine. Sometimes— even when we want something very badly—our loving Heavenly Father responds to our requests by saying "No," and we must accept His answer, even if we don't understand it.

God answers prayers not only according to *our* wishes but also according to *His* master plan. We cannot know that plan, but we can know the Planner . . . and we must trust His wisdom, His righteousness, and His love.

Of this you can be sure: God is listening, and He wants to hear from you now. So what are you waiting for?

When will we realize that we're not troubling
God with our questions and concerns?
His heart is open to hear us—his touch nearer
than our next thought—as if no one in the world
existed but us. Our very personal God
wants to hear from us personally.

Gigi Graham Tchividjian

We get into trouble when we think we *know* what
to do and we stop *asking* God if we're doing it.

Stormie Omartian

God uses our most stumbling, faltering
faith-steps as the open door to His doing for us
"more than we ask or think."

Catherine Marshall

Thought for the Day

Pray about It!
Talk to God often about *every* aspect
of your life . . . He's listening!

More Words from God's Word

*Until now you have not asked for anything
in my name. Ask and you will receive,
so that your joy will be the fullest possible joy.*

John 16:24 NCV

*Do not worry about anything,
but pray and ask God for everything you need,
always giving thanks.*

Philippians 4:6 NCV

Now I Pray

Lord, today I will ask You for the things
I need. In every situation, I will come to you in
prayer. You know what I want, Lord, and more
importantly, You know what I need. Yet even
though I know that You know, I still won't be
too timid—or too busy—to ask.

Amen

Chapter 28

You Are the Light

*You are the light that gives light to the world.
In the same way, you should be a light for
other people. Live so that they will see
the good things you do and will praise
your Father in heaven.*

Matthew 5:14, 16 NCV

How do people know that you're a Christian? Well, you can tell them, of course. And make no mistake about it: *talking* about your faith in God is a very good thing to do. But simply telling people about Jesus isn't enough. You must also be willing to *show* people how a radical Christian (like you) should behave.

Jesus never comes "next." He is always first. And, if you seek to follow Him, you must do so every day of the week, not just on Sundays. After all, you are indeed "the light that gives light to the world," and shouldn't your light shine all the time? Of course it should. God deserves no less, and neither, for that matter, do you.

Your light is the truth of the Gospel message itself
as well as your witness as to Who Jesus is and
what He has done for you.
Don't hide it.

Anne Graham Lotz

Be ye fishers of men. You catch them—
He will clean them.

Anonymous

Thought for the Day

Living Your Life and
Shining Your Light . . .

As a Christian, the most important light
you shine is the light that your own life shines on
the lives of others. May your light shine brightly,
righteously, obediently, and eternally!

More Words from God's Word

We are therefore Christ's ambassadors,
as though God were making his appeal
through us. We implore you on Christ's behalf:
Be reconciled to God.

2 Corinthians 5:20 NIV

But when the Holy Spirit has come upon you,
you will receive power and will tell people about
me everywhere—in Jerusalem, throughout Judea,
in Samaria, and to the ends of the earth.

Acts 1:8 NLT

Now I Pray

Dear Lord, let me share the Good News
of my salvation, and let me tell of Your love and
of Your grace. Make me a faithful ambassador
for You, Father, and make me a witness to
the transforming power of Your Son.
Amen

Chapter 29

Faith for the Future

*Without wavering, let us hold tightly
to the hope we say we have,
for God can be trusted
to keep his promise.*

Hebrews 10:23 NLT

Do you believe that God has wonderful things in store for you? Well, if you're a radical believer, God has plans for you that are so bright that you'd better pack *several* pairs of sunglasses *and* a lifetime supply of sunblock!

The way that you think about your future will play a powerful role in determining how things turn out (it's called the "self-fulfilling prophecy," and it applies to everybody, including you). So here's another question: Are you expecting a terrific tomorrow, or are you dreading a terrible one? The answer to that question will have a powerful impact on the way tomorrow unfolds.

Today, as you live in the present and look to the future, remember that God has an amazing plan for you. Act—and believe—accordingly. And don't forget to pack the sunblock.

Do not limit the limitless God! With Him,
face the future unafraid because
you are never alone.

Mrs. Charles E. Cowman

The best we can hope for in this life is
a knothole peek at the shining realities ahead.
Yet a glimpse is enough. It's enough to convince
our hearts that whatever sufferings and sorrows
currently assail us aren't worthy of comparison
to that which waits over the horizon.

Joni Eareckson Tada

Thought for the Day

For Christians Who Believe
God's Promises . . .

the future is actually too bright to comprehend.

More Words from God's Word

Wisdom is pleasing to you.
If you find it, you have hope for the future.

Proverbs 24:14 NCV

The Lord says, "Forget what happened before,
and do not think about the past.
Look at the new thing I am going to do.
It is already happening. Don't you see it?
I will make a road in
the desert and rivers in the dry land."

Isaiah 43:18-19 NCV

Now I Pray

Dear Lord, as I look to the future, I will place
my trust in You. If I become discouraged,
I will turn to You. If I am afraid, I will seek
strength in You. You are my Father,
and I will place my hope, my trust,
and my faith in You.
Amen

Chapter 30

Making Time for God

Be still, and know that I am God.

Psalm 46:10 NKJV

Face it: We live in a noisy world, a world filled with distractions, frustrations, and complications. But if we allow those distractions to separate us from God's peace, we do ourselves a profound disservice.

Are you one of those busy girls who rush through the day with scarcely a single moment for quiet contemplation and prayer? If so, it's time to reorder your priorities.

Nothing is more important than the time you spend with your Savior. So be still and claim the inner peace that is your spiritual birthright: the peace of Jesus Christ. It is offered freely; it has been paid for in full; it is yours for the asking. So ask. And then share.

The many rewards of a serious,
consistent prayer life demonstrate clearly
that time with our Lord should be our first priority.

Shirley Dobson

An early walk and talk with the Lord
will last all day.

Anonymous

Thought for the Day

The Right Way to Start the Day:

Begin each day with a few minutes of quiet time
to organize your thoughts. During this time,
read at least one uplifting passage and thus
begin your day on a positive, productive note.

More Words from God's Word

In quietness and trust is your strength.

Isaiah 30:15 NASB

I wait quietly before God,
for my salvation comes from him.

Psalm 62:1 NLT

Now I Pray

Lord, Your Word is my light; I will study it,
trust it, and share it with all who cross
my path. I will turn to You, Father,
in the quiet moments of the day.
And, I will seek to share the Good News
of Your perfect Son and Your perfect Word.

Amen

Chapter 31

For God So Loved the World

For God so loved the world that he gave
his only Son, so that everyone
who believes in him will not perish
but have eternal life.

John 3:16 NLT

make no mistake about it: God loves our world. He loves it so much, in fact, that He sent His only begotten Son to die for our sins. And now we, as believers, are challenged to return God's love by obeying His commandments and honoring His Son.

When you open your heart and accept God's love, you are transformed not just for today, but for all eternity. When you accept the Father's love, you feel differently about yourself, your world, your neighbors, your family, and your church. When you experience God's presence and invite His Son into your heart, you feel the need to share His message and to obey His commandments.

God loved this world so much that He sent His Son to save it. And now only one real question remains for you: what will you do in response to God's love? The answer should be obvious: If you haven't already done so, accept Jesus Christ as Your Savior. He's waiting patiently for you, but please don't make Him wait another minute longer.

I am convinced our hearts are not healthy
until they have been satisfied by
the only completely healthy love that exists:
the love of God Himself.

Beth Moore

Accepting God's love as a gift instead of trying
to earn it had somehow seemed presumptuous
and arrogant to me, when, in fact, my pride was
tricking me into thinking that I could merit
His love and forgiveness with my own strength.

Lisa Whelchel

Thought for the Day

God's Love Is
Our Greatest Security Blanket:
Kay Arthur advises, "Snuggle in God's arms.
When you are hurting, when you feel lonely
or left out, let Him cradle you, comfort you,
reassure you of His all-sufficient power
and love." Enough said.

More Words from God's Word

We know how much God loves us,
and we have put our trust in him.
God is love, and all who live in love live in God,
and God lives in them.

1 John 4:16 NLT

The unfailing love of the LORD never ends!

Lamentations 3:22 NLT

Now I Pray

Dear God, the Bible teaches me that Your love
lasts forever. Thank You, God, for Your love.
Let me trust Your promises,
and let me live according to Your teachings,
not just for today, but forever.

Amen

Even More Words from Words from God's Word

(And Words to Live by Too)

The New You

I will give you a new heart
and put a new spirit within you.

Ezekiel 36:26 NKJV

The Lord says, "Forget what happened before,
and do not think about the past.
Look at the new thing I am going to do.
It is already happening. Don't you see it?
I will make a road in the desert
and rivers in the dry land."

Isaiah 43:18-19 NCV

create in me a clean heart, O God,
and renew a steadfast spirit within me.

Psalm 51:10 NKJV

God wants to
revolutionize our
lives—by showing us
how knowing Him can
be the most powerful
force to help us
become all
we want to be.

—

Bill Hybels

*Faith does not struggle;
faith lets God do it all.*

—

Corrie ten Boom

The Power of Faith

Have faith in the LORD your God
and you will be upheld; have faith in his prophets
and you will be successful.

2 Chronicles 20:20 NIV

I tell you the truth, you can say to this mountain,
"Go, fall into the sea." And if you have
no doubts in your mind and believe that
what you say will happen,
God will do it for you.

Mark 11:23 NCV

Anything is possible if a person believes.

Mark 9:23 NLT

God Loves You

We love Him because He first loved us.

1 John 4:19 NKJV

That is, in Christ, he chose us before
the world was made so that we would be
his holy people—people without blame
before him. Because of his love,
God had already decided to make us
his own children through Jesus Christ.
That was what he wanted and what pleased him.

Ephesians 1:4-5 NCV

His banner over me was love.

Song of Solomon 2:4 KJV

Everything I possess
of any worth is
a direct product of God's love.
—
Beth Moore

Only the truly forgiven
are truly forgiving.
–
C. S. Lewis

Forgiveness

And be kind and compassionate to one another,
forgiving one another,
just as God also forgave you in Christ.

Ephesians 4:32 HCSB

In prayer there is a connection between
what God does and what you do.
You can't get forgiveness from God, for instance,
without also forgiving others.
If you refuse to do your part,
you cut yourself off from God's part.

Matthew 6:14-15 MSG

If someone does wrong to you,
do not pay him back by doing wrong to him.
Try to do what everyone thinks is right.

Romans 12:17 NCV

Living Courageously

*Be strong and brave, and do the work.
Don't be afraid or discouraged,
because the Lord God, my God, is with you.
He will not fail you or leave you.*

1 Chronicles 28:20 NCV

**Do not be afraid . . .
I am your shield, your very great reward.**

Genesis 15:1 NIV

But He said to them, "It is I. Don't be afraid!"

John 6:20 HCSB

*Let not
your heart be
troubled . . .*

John 14:1 KJV

When you extend hospitality
to others, you're not trying
to impress people,
you're trying to reflect
God to them.

—

Max Lucado

Kindness

*Kind people do themselves a favor,
but cruel people bring trouble on themselves.*

Proverbs 11:17 NCV

**"Whatever you did for one of the least
of these brothers of Mine,
you did for Me."**

Matthew 25:40 HCSB

*And may the Lord cause you to increase and
overflow with love for one another and
for everyone, just as we also do for you.*

1 Thessalonians 3:12

Attitude

Finally brothers, whatever is true, whatever is honorable, whatever is just, whatever is pure, whatever is lovely, whatever is commendable— if there is any moral excellence and if there is any praise—dwell on these things.

Philippians 4:8 HCSB

Your attitude should be the same as that of Christ Jesus: Who, being in very nature God, did not consider equality with God something to be grasped, but made himself nothing, taking the very nature of a servant, being made in human likeness. And being found in appearance as a man, he humbled himself and became obedient to death—even death on a cross!

Philippians 2:5-8

Those who are pure in their thinking are happy, because they will be with God.

Matthew 5:8 NCV

Life is 10% what happens to you and 90% how you respond to it.
—
Charles Swindoll

He who walks
with the wise
grows wise,
but a companion
of fools
suffers harm.

-

Proverbs 13:20 NIV

Wise Choices

But if any of you needs wisdom,
you should ask God for it.
He is generous and enjoys giving to all people,
so he will give you wisdom.

James 1:5 NCV

*Understanding is like a fountain
which gives life to those who use it.*
Proverbs 16:22 NCV

**But wisdom will help you be good
and do what is right.**

Proverbs 2:20 NCV

Spiritual Maturity

Grow in grace and understanding of
our Master and Savior, Jesus Christ.
Glory to the Master, now and forever! Yes!

2 Peter 3:18 MSG

When I was a child, I spoke and thought
and reasoned as a child does.
But when I grew up, I put away childish things.

1 Corinthians 13:11 NLT

Therefore let us leave the elementary
teachings about Christ
and go on to maturity ...

Hebrews 6:1 NIV

God's goal is that we
move toward maturity—
all our past failures and
faults notwithstanding.

—

Charles Swindoll

a believer
comes to christ;
a disciple
follows after him.
—
vance hauner

Following Christ

**And when He had spoken this,
He said to him,
"Follow Me."**

John 21:19 NKJV

Whoever serves me must follow me.
Then my servant will be with me everywhere I am.
My Father will honor anyone who serves me.

John 12:26 NCV

For this is the secret: Christ lives in you,
and this is your assurance
that you will share in his glory.

Colossians 1:27 NLT

Let the peace of Christ
rule in your hearts,
since as members of
one body you were
called to peace.
And be thankful.

—

Colossians 3:15 NIV